HAL•LEONARD®
PIANO PLAY-ALONG

AUDIO
ACCESS
INCLUDED

PLAYBACK+
Speed • Pitch • Balance • Loop

PIANO | VOCAL | GUITAR • AUDIO   VOLUME 117

ALICIA KEYS

Cover photo courtesy ABC/Photofest ©ABC
Photographer: Craig Sjodin

ISBN 978-1-4584-1574-5

HAL•LEONARD®
CORPORATION
7777 W. BLUEMOUND RD. P.O. BOX 13819 MILWAUKEE, WI 53213

In Australia Contact:
Hal Leonard Australia Pty. Ltd.
4 Lentara Court
Cheltenham, Victoria, 3192 Australia
Email: ausadmin@halleonard.com.au

Visit Hal Leonard Online at
www.halleonard.com

CONTENTS

PAGE TITLE

EMPIRE STATE OF MIND

Words and Music by ALICIA KEYS, SHAWN CARTER,
JANE'T SEWELL, ANGELA HUNTE, AL SHUCKBURGH,
BERT KEYES and SYLVIA ROBINSON

Moderate Hip-Hop

1. Yeah, yeah, I'm up at Brook- lyn, now I'm down in Tri- bec- a, right next to De
2., 3. (See Rap lyrics)

Ni- ro, but I'll be hood for- ev- er. I'm the new Si-

* Recorded a half step higher.

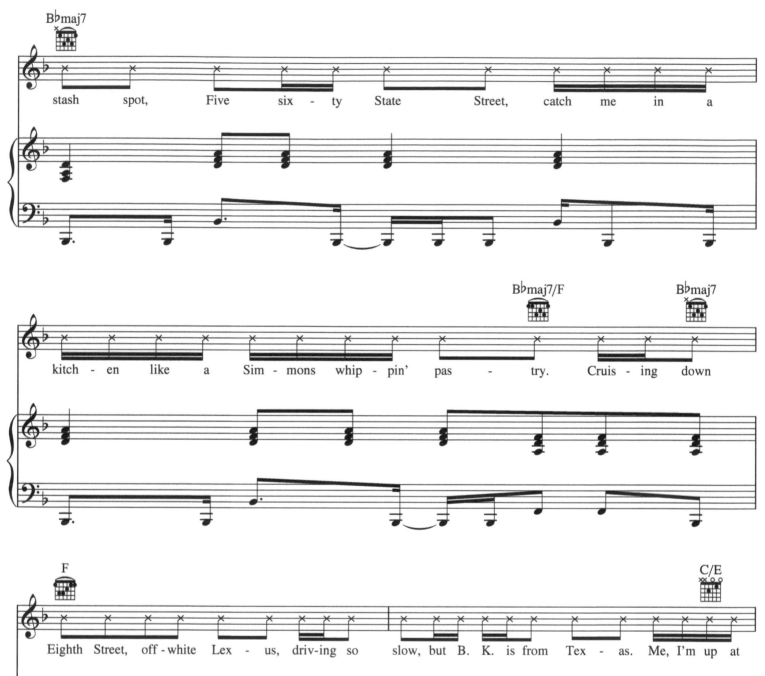

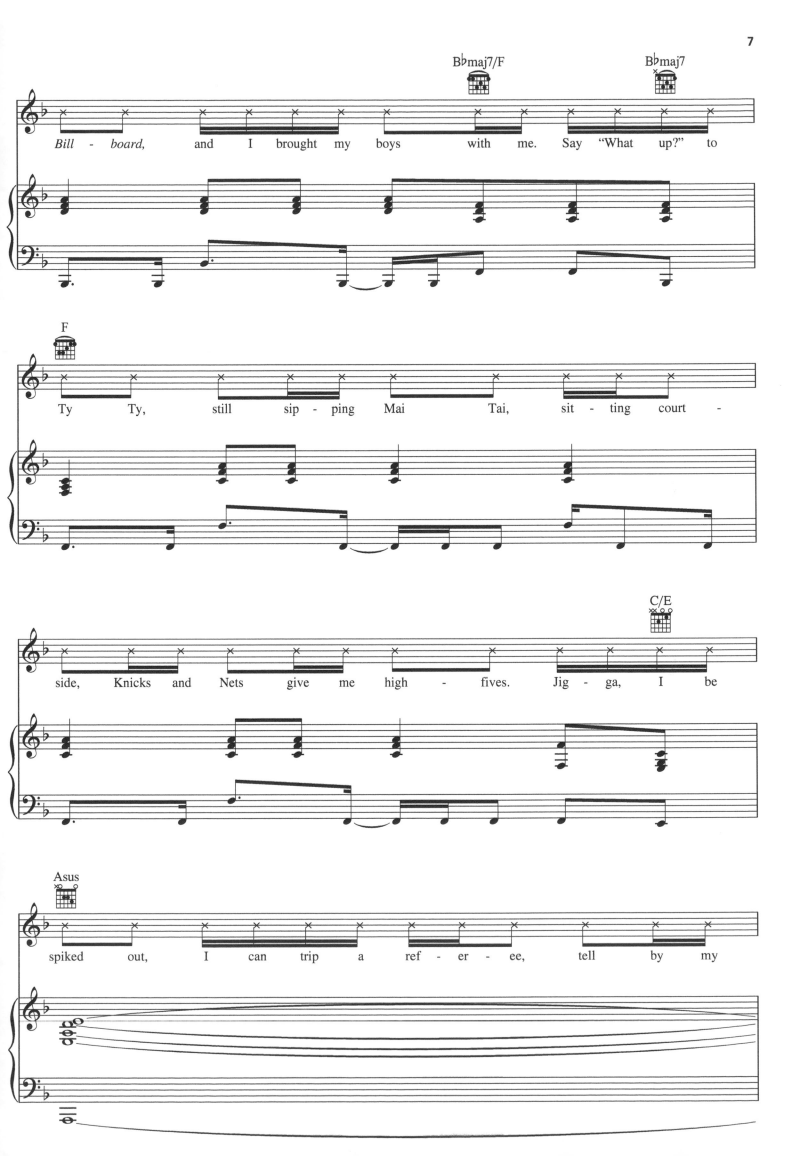

To Coda ⊕

re you. ___ Let's here it for New ___ York, New ___ York, New ___

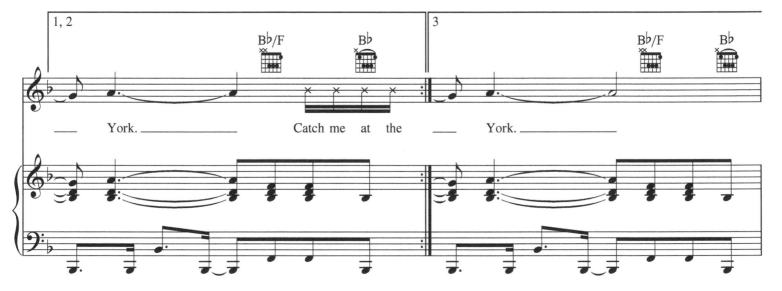

1, 2
___ York. _____ Catch me at the ___

3
___ York. _____

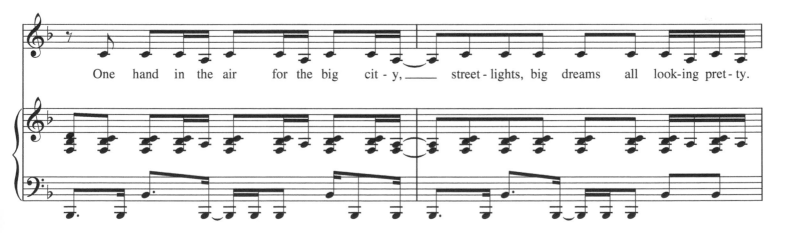

One hand in the air for the big cit - y, ___ street - lights, big dreams all look-ing pret - ty.

No place __ in the world that can com - pare, put your light-ers in the air, ev-'ry-bod-y say __

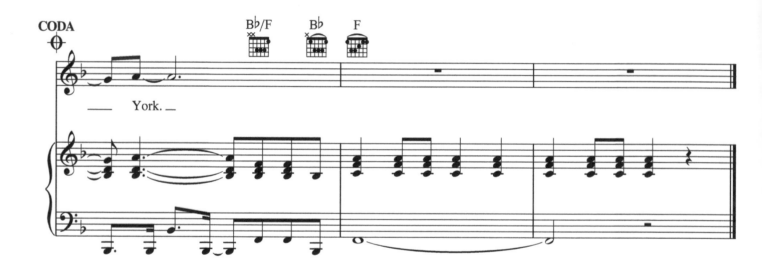

Rap Lyrics

2. Catch me at the X with OG at a Yankee game.
   Dude, I made the Yankee hat more famous than a Yankee can.
   You should know I bleed blue, but I ain't a crip though,
   But I got a gang of brothas walking with my clique though.

   Welcome to the melting pot, corners where we selling rocks,
   Afrika bambaataa, home of the hip-hop,
   Yellow cab, gypsy cab, dollar cab, holla back,
   For foreigners it ain't for they act like they forgot how to act.

   Eight million stories out there and they're naked.
   City, it's a pity half of y'all won't make it.
   Me, I gotta plug Special Ed, I got it made,
   If Jeezy's paying LeBron, I'm paying Dwyane Wade.

   3 dice, Cee Lo, 3-Card Monte,
   Labor Day parade, rest in peace Bob Marley.
   Statue of Liberty, long live the World Trade,
   Long live the King, yo, I'm from the Empire State that's...

3. Lights is blinding, girls need blinders
   So they can step out of bounds quick.
   The sidelines is blind with casualties, who sip your life casually,
   Then gradually become worse. Don't bite the apple, Eve.

   Caught up in the in-crowd, now you're in style,
   And in the winter gets cold, en vogue with your skin out.
   The city of sin is a pity on a whim,
   Good girls gone bad, the city's filled with them.

   Mami took a bus trip, now she got her bust out,
   Everybody ride her, just like a bus route.
   Hail Mary to the city, you're a virgin,
   And Jesus can't save you, life starts when the church in.

   Came here for school, graduated to the high life.
   Ball players, rap stars, addicted to the limelight.
   MD, MA got you feeling like a champion,
   The city never sleeps, better slip you a Ambien.

FALLIN'

Words and Music by
ALICIA KEYS

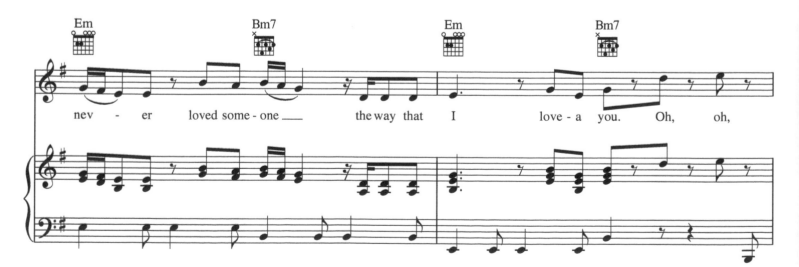

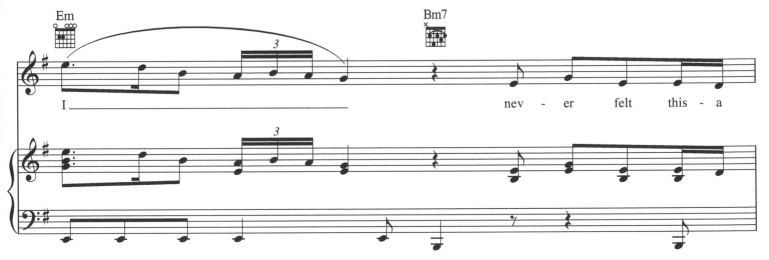

I _____ nev - er felt this - a

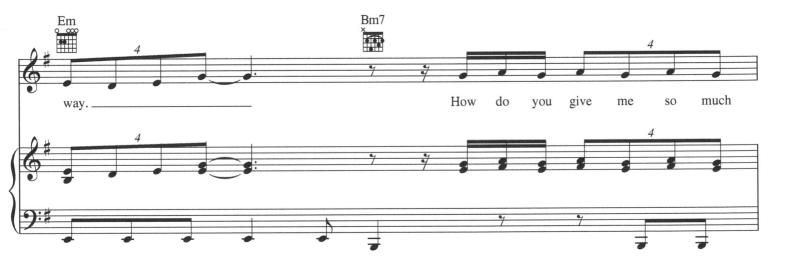

way. _____ How do you give me so much

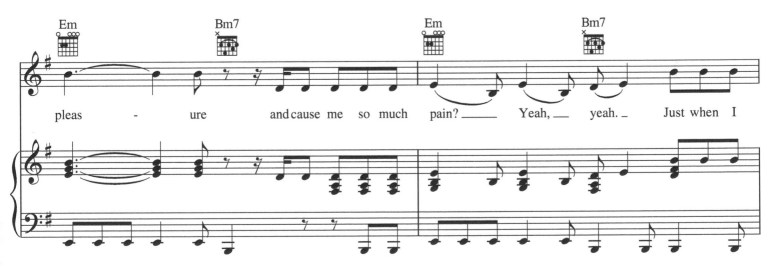

pleas - ure and cause me so much pain? _____ Yeah, ___ yeah. _ Just when I

think _____ I'm tak-ing more than would a fool, _____ I ____ start

fall - in' ___ back in love with you ___ I ___ keep ___ on

fall - in' in and out ___ of love with - a you. I ___

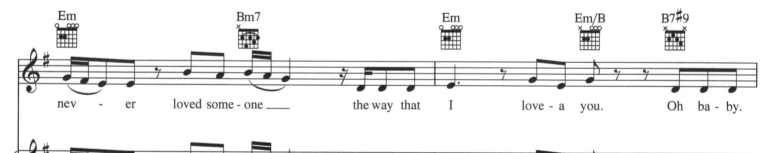

nev - er loved some - one ___ the way that I love - a you. Oh ba - by.

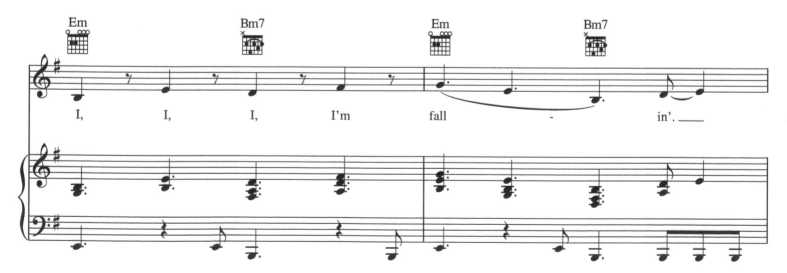

I, I, I, I'm fall - in'. ___

I, I, I, I'm fall - in'.

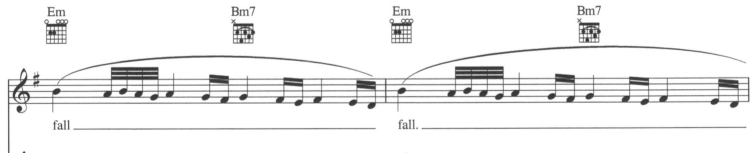

Fall

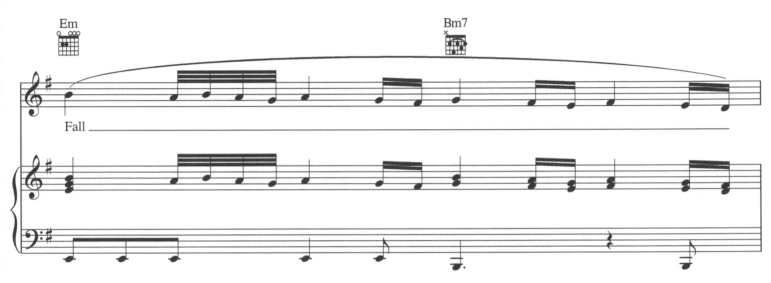

fall   fall.

I keep on fall - in' in and out of

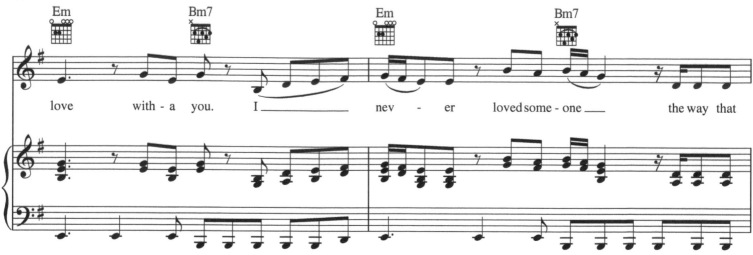

love   with - a   you.   I _____ nev - er   loved some - one ____ the way that

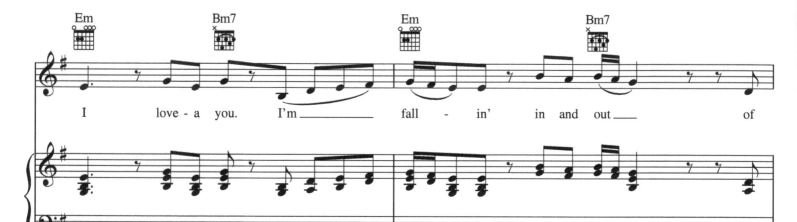

I   love - a   you.   I'm _____ fall - in'   in   and   out ____ of

love   with - a   you.   I _____ nev - er   loved some - one ____ the way that

I   love - a   you.   I'm _____ fall - in'   in   and   out ____ of

love   with - a you.   I _____ nev - er   loved some - one _____   the way that

I   love - a you.   What?

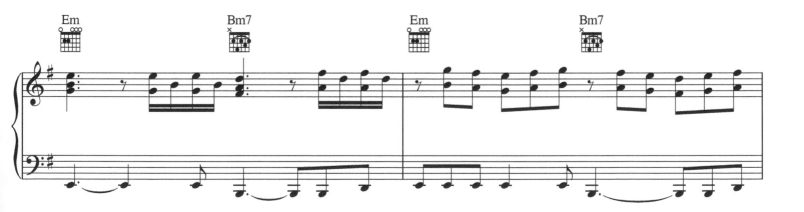

IF I AIN'T GOT YOU

Words and Music by
ALICIA KEYS

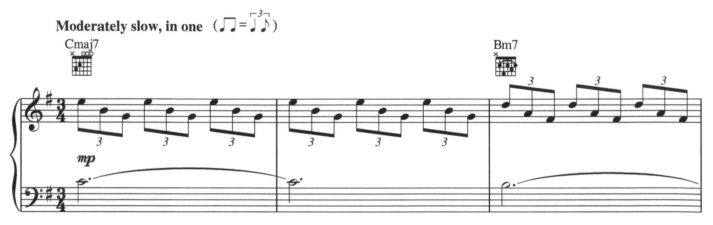

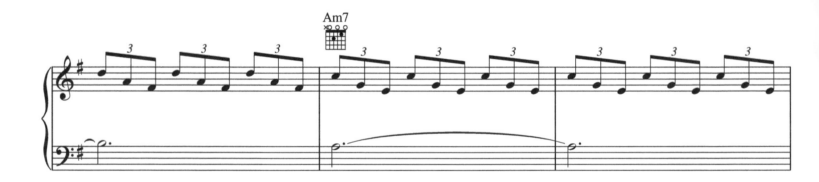

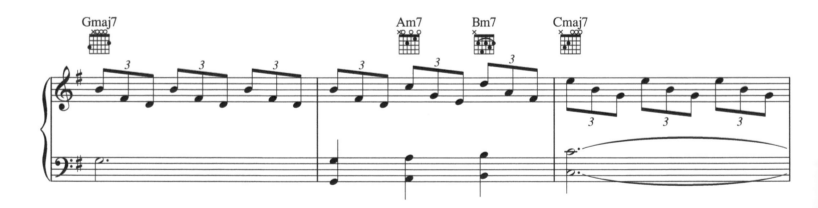

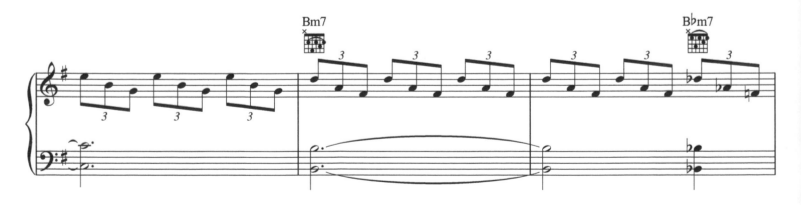

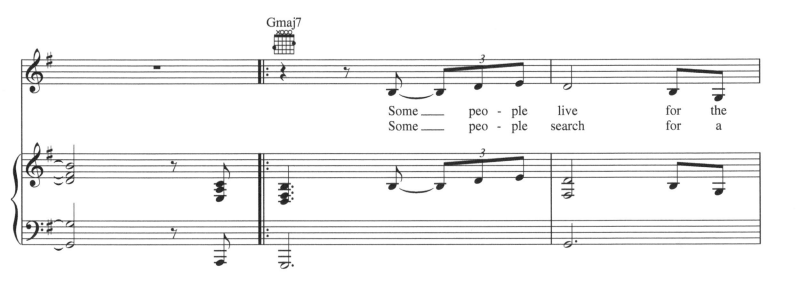

Some ___ peo - ple live ___ for the
Some ___ peo - ple search ___ for a

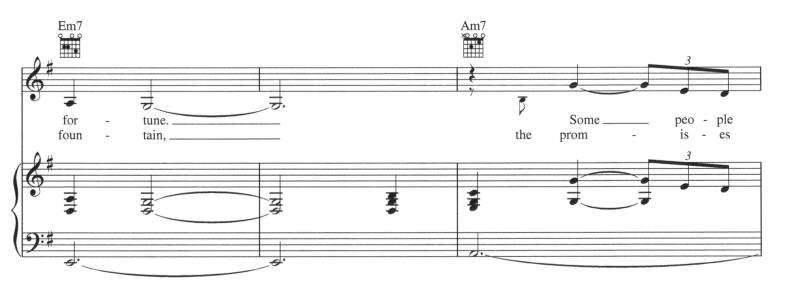

for - tune. _____ Some _____ peo - ple
foun - tain, _____ the prom - is - es

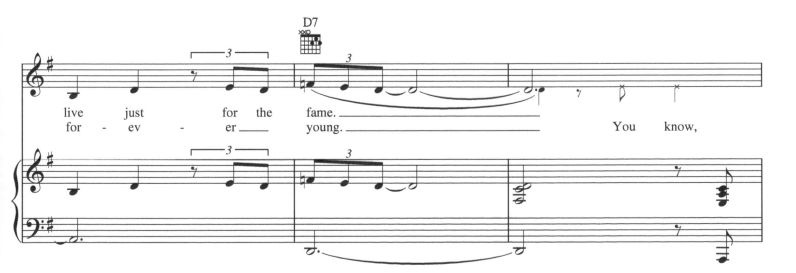

live just for the fame. _____
for - ev - er ___ young. _____ You know,

Some ___ peo - ple live for the pow - er, ___
some ___ peo - ple need three doz - en ros -

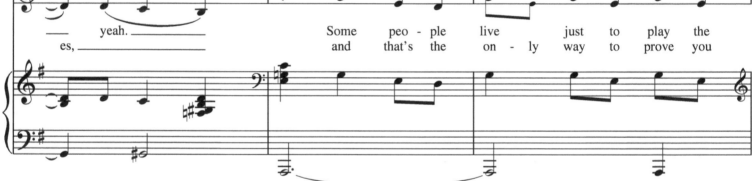

___ yeah. _____ Some peo - ple live just to play the
es, _____ and that's the on - ly way to prove you

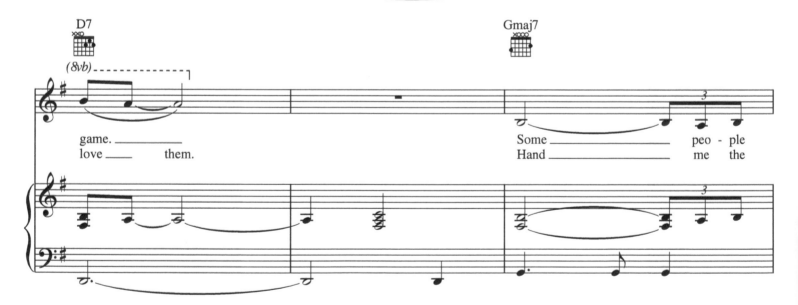

game. _____ Some _____ peo - ple
love ___ them. Hand _____ me the

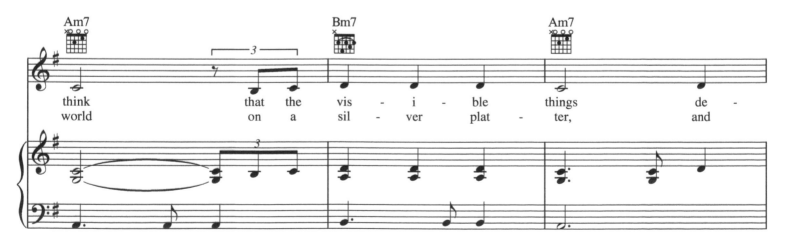

think that the vis - i - ble things de -
world on a sil - ver plat - ter, and

fine _____ what's with - in. _____
what _____ good would it be _____

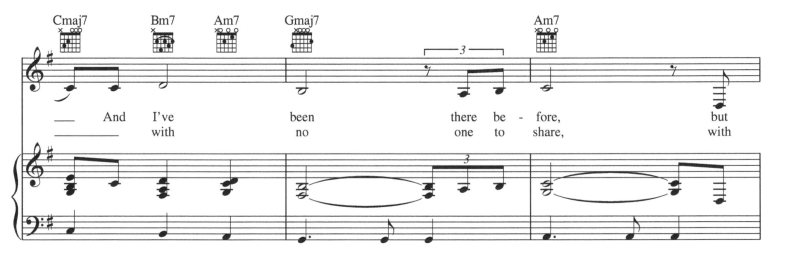

_____ And I've been there be - fore, but
_____ with no one to share, with

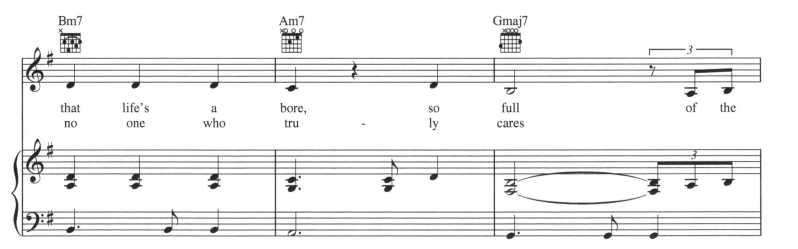

that life's a bore, so full of the
no one who tru - ly cares

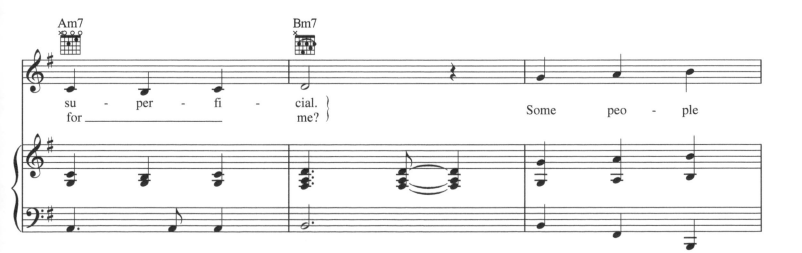

su - per - fi - cial. } Some peo - ple
for _____ me? }

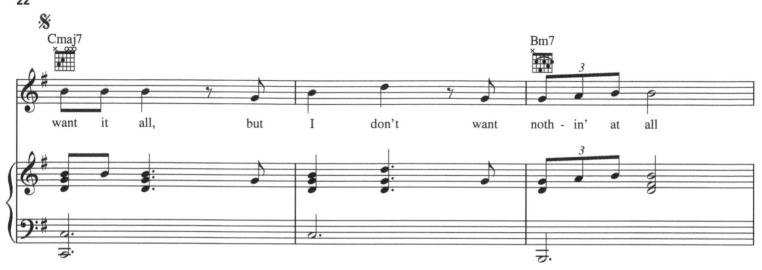

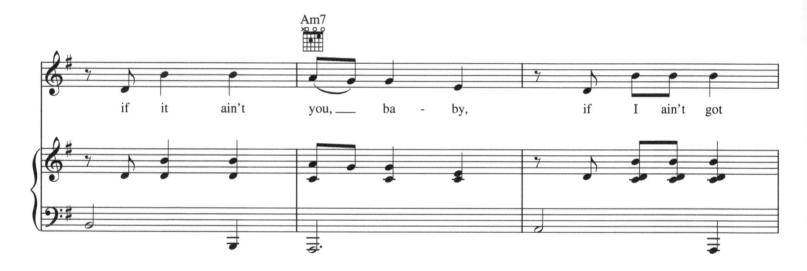

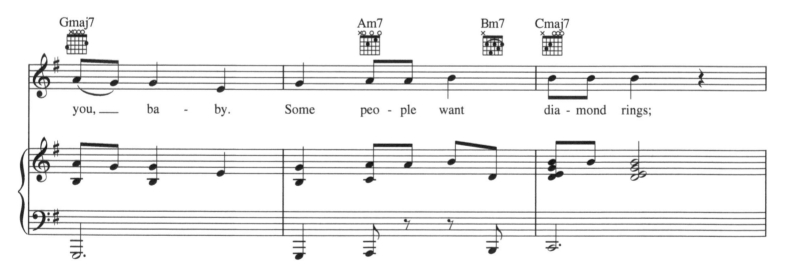

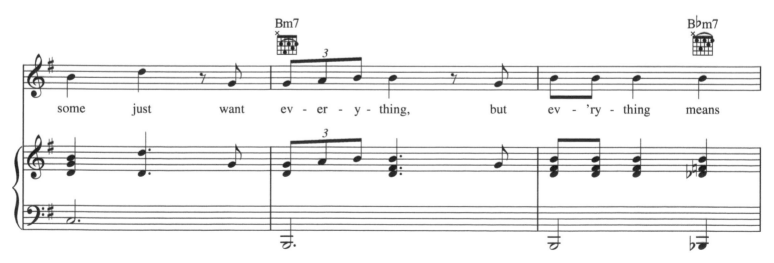

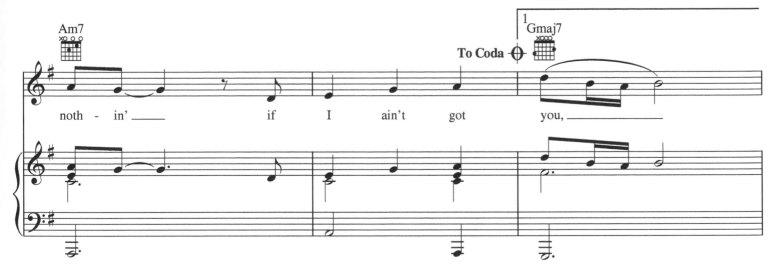

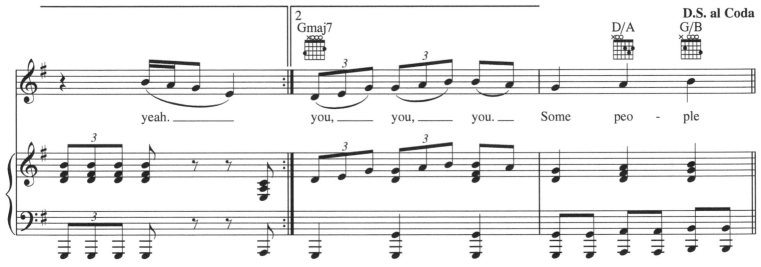

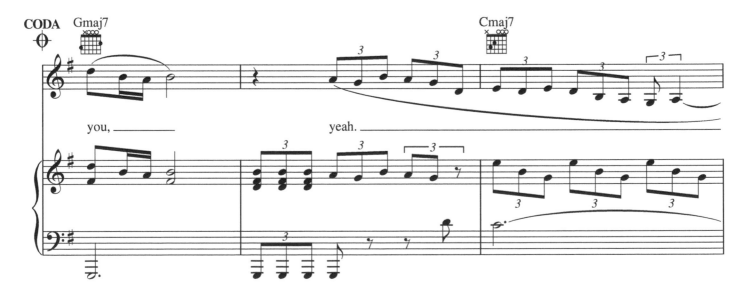

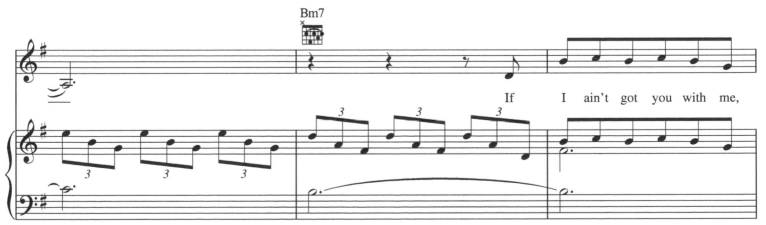

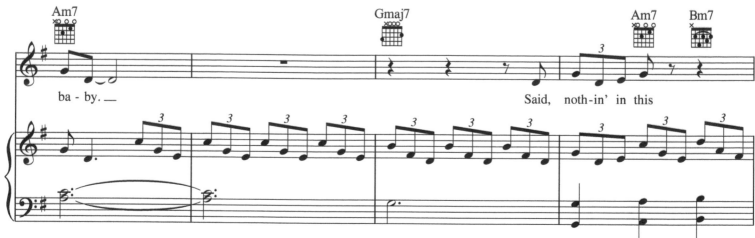

ba - by. ___ Said, noth-in' in this

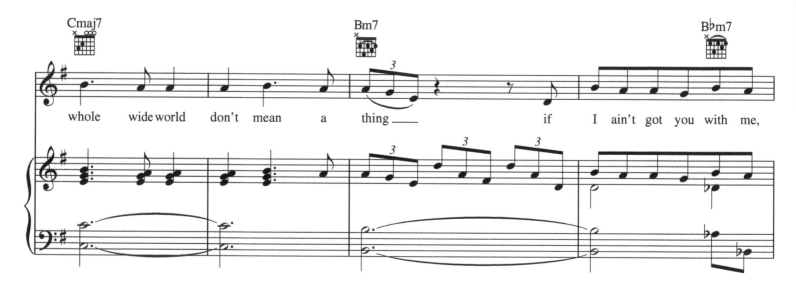

whole wide world don't mean a thing ___ if I ain't got you with me,

ba - by. ___

rit.

Freely

NO ONE

Words and Music by ALICIA KEYS,
KERRY BROTHERS, JR. and GEORGE HARRY

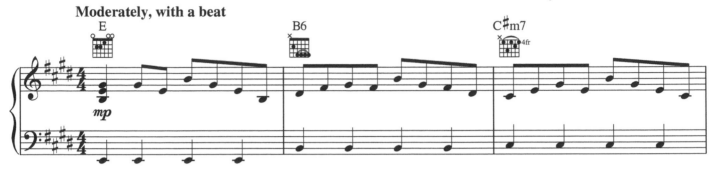

I just want you close

where you can stay ___ for - ev - er. ___ You ___ can be ___

___ sure ___ that it will on - ly get bet - ter. ___

You __ and me to-geth - er _____ through the days and nights. _____

__ I don't wor - ry 'cause __ ev -'ry-thing's gon - na be al - right. __

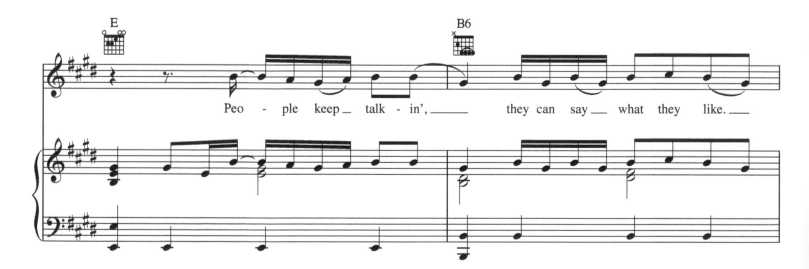

Peo - ple keep __ talk - in', _____ they can say __ what they like. __

But __ all I know __ is ev-'ry-thing's gon-na be al - right. _____ And no __ one, no __

one, no one can get in the way of what I'm feel - in'.

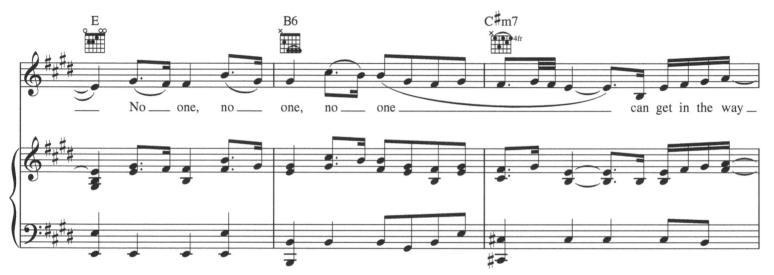

No one, no one, no one can get in the way

of what I feel for you, you, you,

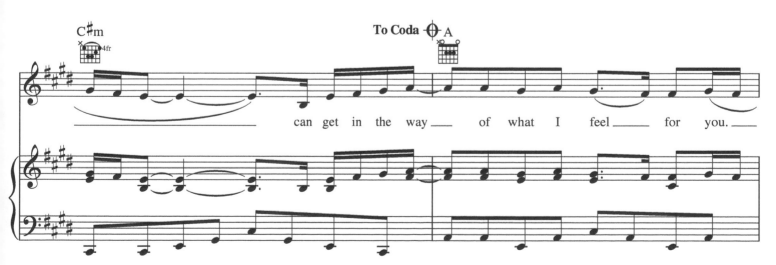

can get in the way of what I feel for you.

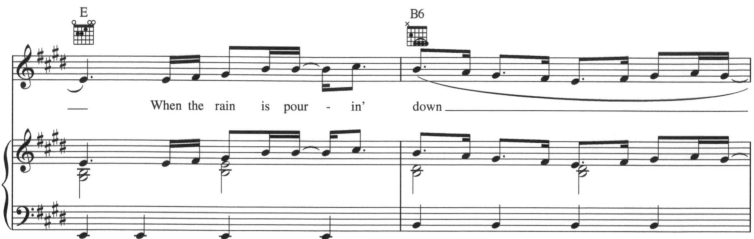

When the rain is pour - in' down _____

_____ and my heart is hurt - in', _____ you will al - ways _ be a-

round. _____ This I know for cer - tain. _____

D.S. al Coda

CODA

_____ of what I feel. _____ I know _____ some peo - ple

search the world to find _____ some-thin' like what we have. _____ I

know _____ peo-ple will try, try to di-vide some-thin' so real. _____ So, 'til the

end of time, I'm tell-ing you there ain't no one, _____ no _____ one, no _____ one _____

_____ can get in the way _____ of what I'm feel - in'. _____

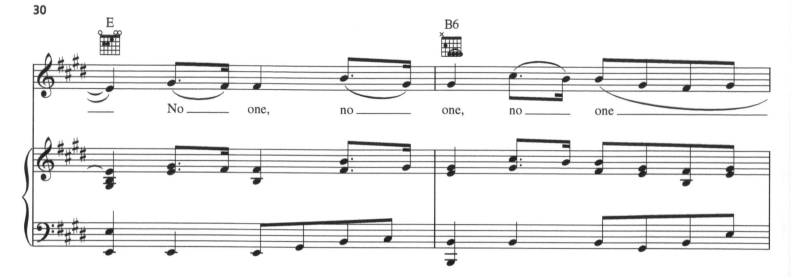

No ___ one, no ___ one, no ___ one ___

___ can get in the way ___ of what I feel ___ for you. ___

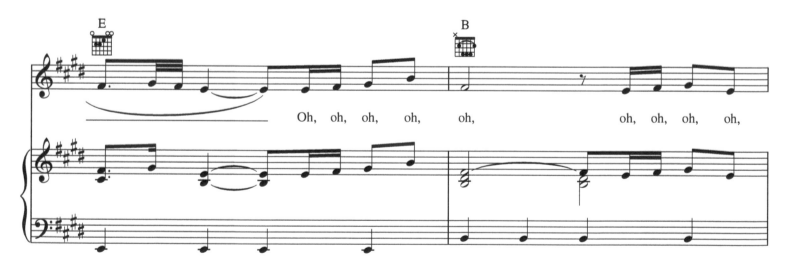

___ Oh, oh, oh, oh, oh, oh, oh, oh, oh,

oh, oh, oh, oh, oh, oh, ho, oh, ho, oh, ho, oh, ho, oh. ___ Oh, oh, oh, oh,

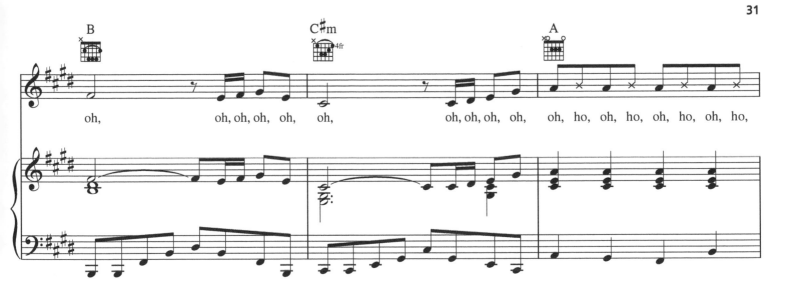

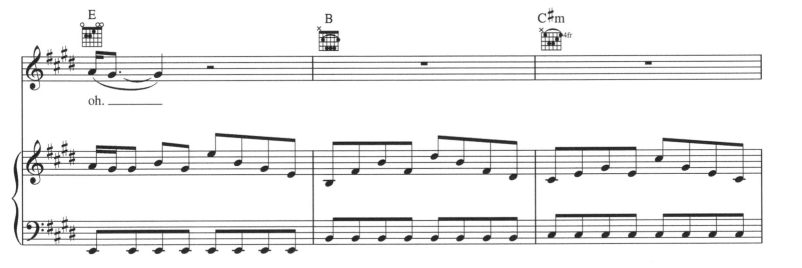

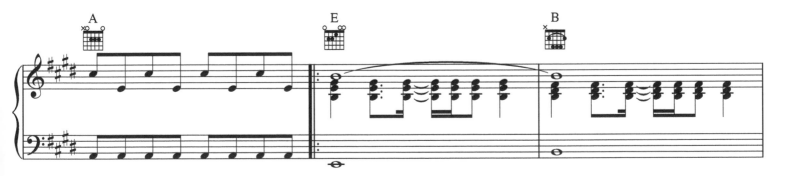

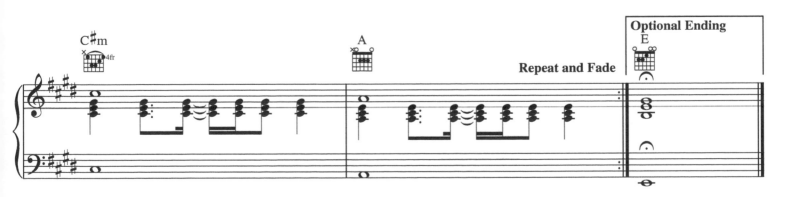

LIKE YOU'LL NEVER SEE ME AGAIN

Words and Music by ALICIA KEYS
and KERRY BROTHERS, JR.

Relaxed R&B Ballad

If I had no more time, no more time left to be here, ___

___ would you cher - ish what we had? Was it ev - 'ry - thing ___ that you were look-ing
Do you know un - til you lose it, that it's ev - 'ry - thing ___ that we are look-ing

for?   If I could-n't feel your touch   and no long - er were you with me, _
for?   When I wake up in the morn-ing,   you're be-side   me. _

_   I'd be wish - ing you were here, to be ev - 'ry - thing _ that   I'd be look-ing
_   I'm so thank - ful that I found ev - 'ry - thing _ that I've been look-ing

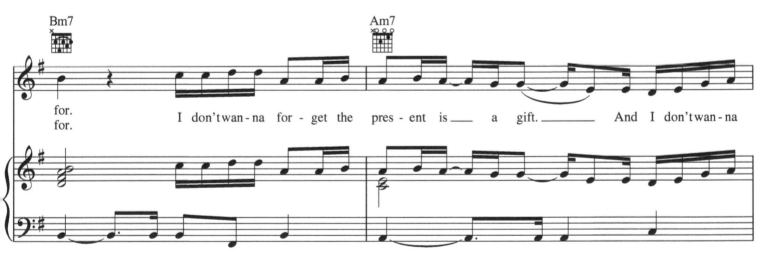

for.   I don't wan - na for - get the pres - ent is _ a gift. _____ And I don't wan - na
for.

take for grant - ed the time you may have here with me. _____ 'Cause Lord _ on - ly

knows an-oth-er day is not real-ly guar-an-teed. _____ So ev-'ry time you

hold me, hold me like this is the last time. Ev-'ry time you

kiss me, kiss me like you'll nev-er see me a-gain. _____ Ev-'ry time you

touch me, touch me like this is the last time. Prom-ise that you'll

love me,   love me like you'll nev - er see me a - gain, _____ oh, oh, oh. __

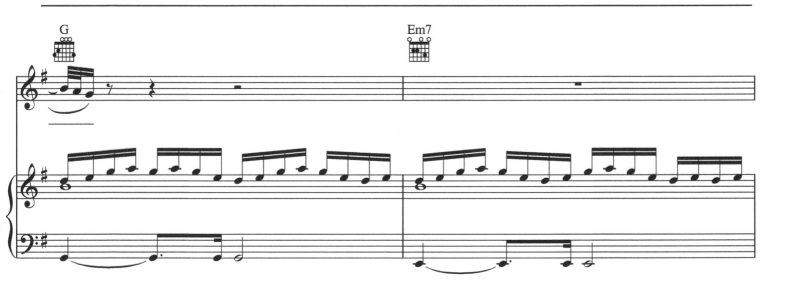

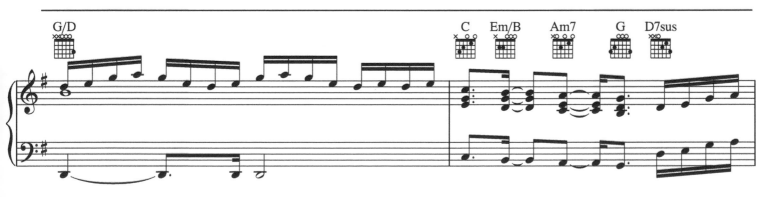

How _ man-y real-ly know what love is? _____ Mil - lions nev - er will.

never see me again. _____ So ev-'ry time you hold me, hold me like this is the
Add lead vocal ad lib.

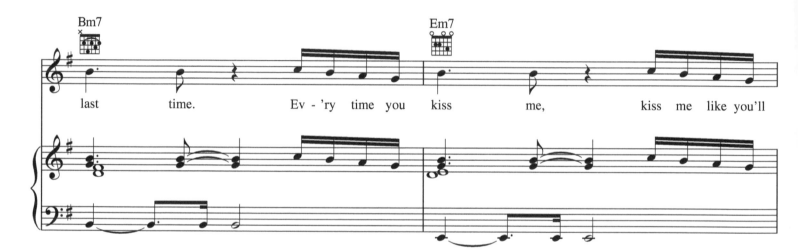

last time. Ev-'ry time you kiss me, kiss me like you'll

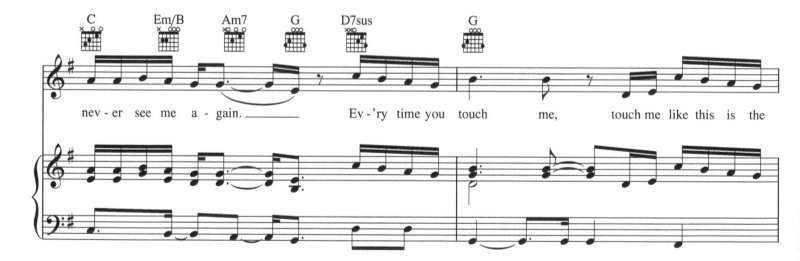

nev-er see me a-gain. _____ Ev-'ry time you touch me, touch me like this is the

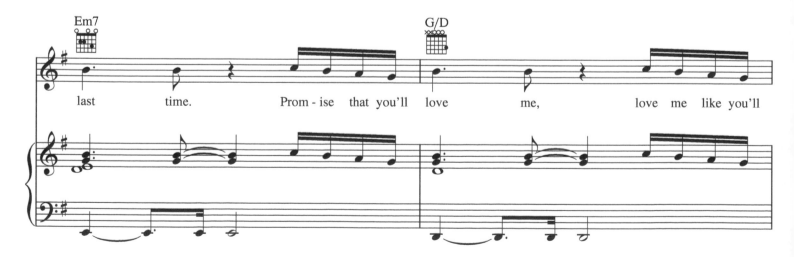

last time. Prom-ise that you'll love me, love me like you'll

nev-er see me a-gain, _____ oh, oh, oh. (Oh, ___ oh, _____ oh.) _____
End vocal ad lib.

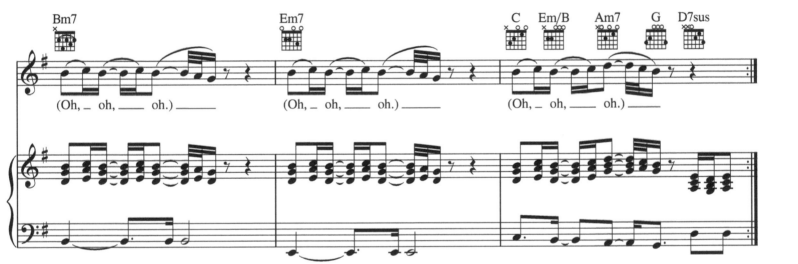

(Oh, _ oh, _____ oh.) _____   (Oh, _ oh, _____ oh.) _____   (Oh, _ oh, _____ oh.) _____

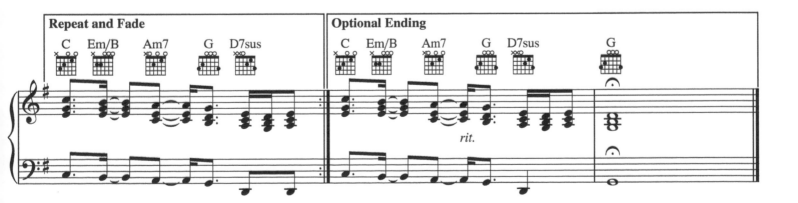

Repeat and Fade   **Optional Ending**

rit.

TRY SLEEPING
WITH A BROKEN HEART

Words and Music by ALICIA KEYS,
JEFF BHASKER and PATRICK REYNOLDS

I'm gon-na find a way to make _____ it _____ with - out you. _____

I'm gon - na hold on to the times _____ that _____ we had. To -

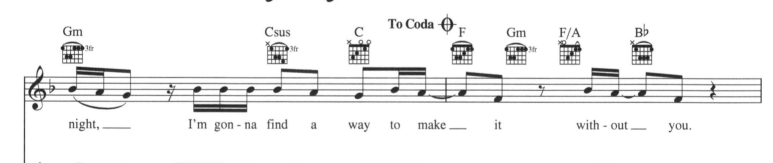

To Coda

night, _____ I'm gon - na find a way to make _____ it with - out _____ you.

Have you ev - er tried sleep-in' with a bro - ken heart? _____ Well, you could try sleep - in' in my

in. Take me; make me. You know that I'll al - ways be in

D.S. al Coda

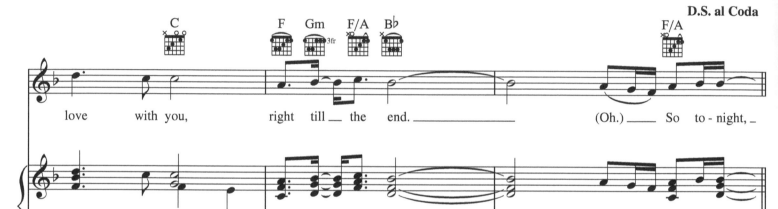

love with you, right till the end. _____ (Oh.) _____ So to - night, _____

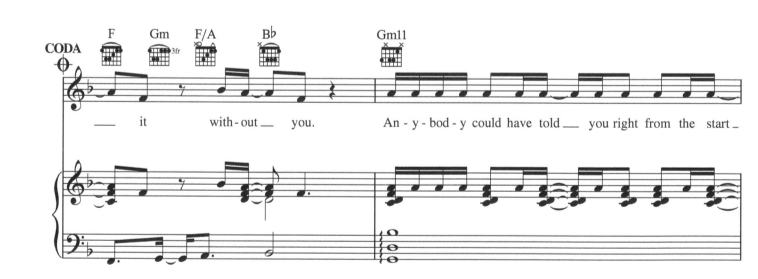

CODA

_____ it with - out _____ you. An - y - bod - y could have told _____ you right from the start _____

_____ it's 'bout to fall a - part. _____ So rath - er than hold on to a bro - ken dream, _____

I'll — just hold on — to love. And I could find a way to make —

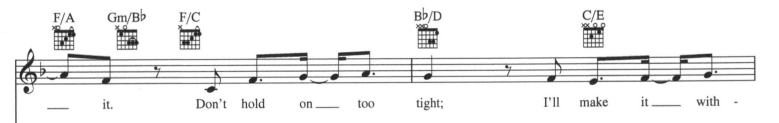

— it. Don't hold on — too tight; I'll make it — with -

out you — to-night. So to - night, — I wan - na find a way to make —

— it with - out — you. To - night, — I'm gon - na find a way to make —

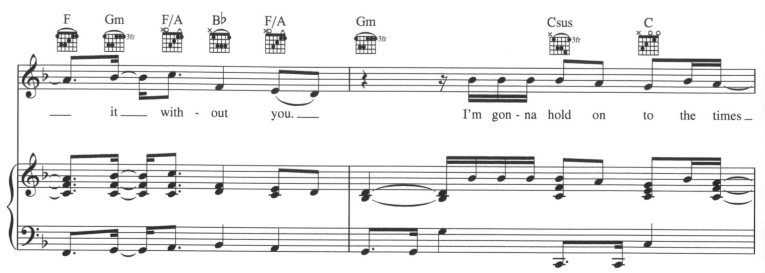

La

la   la   la   la la la   la,   la   la la la la   la   la,   la   la la la la   la

la   la   la   la   la   la   la   la,   la   la   la   la   la   la.

A WOMAN'S WORTH

Words and Music by ALICIA KEYS
and ERIKA ROSE

Moderately slow

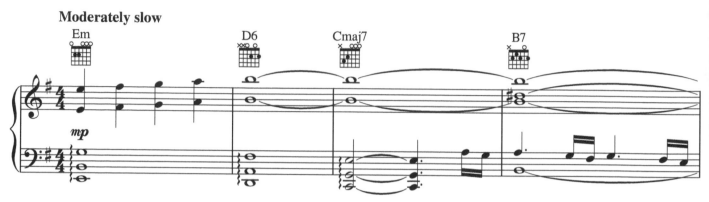

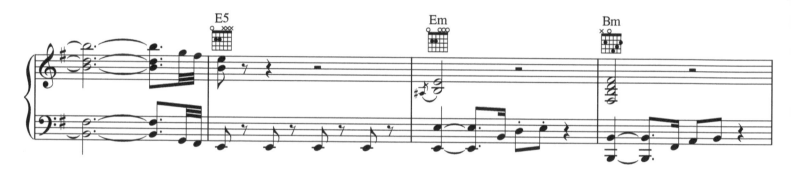

You could buy me dia - monds, you could buy me
fair - ly, I'll give you all my

pearls, _____ take me on a cruise a - round _ the world. _____ (Ba-
goods; _____ treat you like a real _ wom - an should. _____ (Ba-

Bm7   Em

- by, you _ know I'm _ worth it.) Din - ner lit by can - dles,   run my bub - ble
- by, I _ know you're _ worth it.) If you nev - er play me,   prom - ise not to

Bm   Am7

bath, _____ make love ten - der - ly to last _ and last. _____ (Ba-
bluff, _____ I'll hold you down when shit _ gets rough. _____ (Ba-

Bm7   Am   G6   D/F#   Em

- by, you _ know I'm _ worth it.) Wan - na please, wan - na keep, wan - na treat your wom - an
- by, I _ know you're _ worth it.) She _ walks the _ mile makes you smile, all the while be - ing

D   Am   G6   D/F#   Em

right.   Not just dough, but a show that you know she is worth your
true.   Don't _ take for _ grant - ed the pas - sions that she has for

time.}
you.}
You will lose if you choose to re-fuse to put her

first.
She will, if she can, find a man who knows her

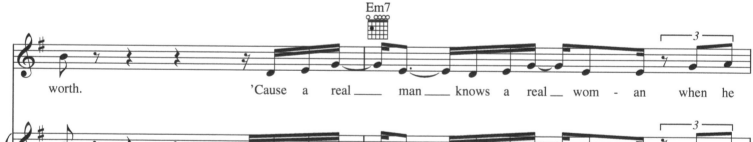

worth.
'Cause a real man knows a real wom-an when he

sees her,
and a real wom-an knows a real man

a wom - an's worth. No need to read be-tween the lines spelled out for you. Just

hear this song, 'cause you can't go wrong when you val - ue a

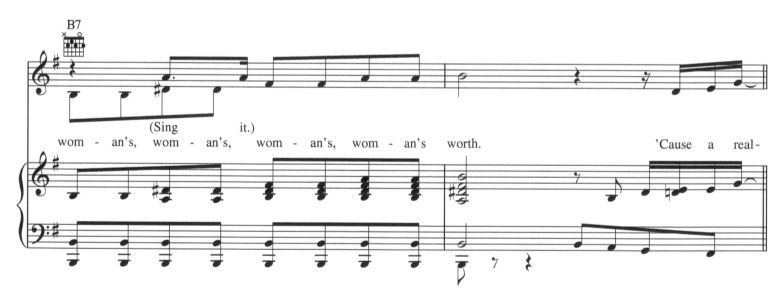

(Sing it.)

wom - an's, wom - an's, wom - an's, wom - an's worth. 'Cause a real-

— man — knows a real — wom - an when he sees her, and a real —

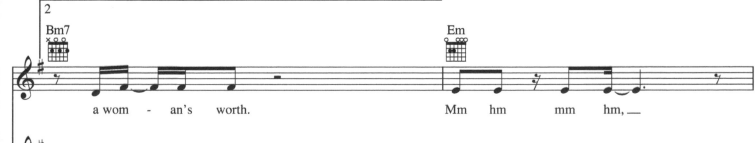

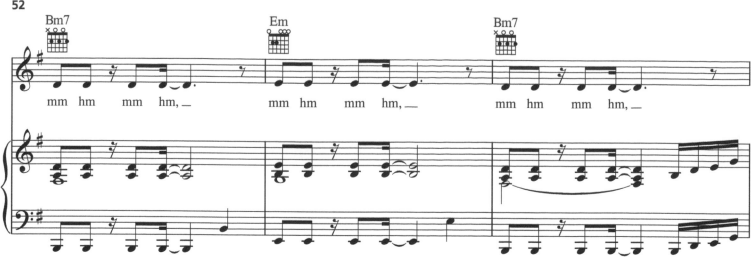

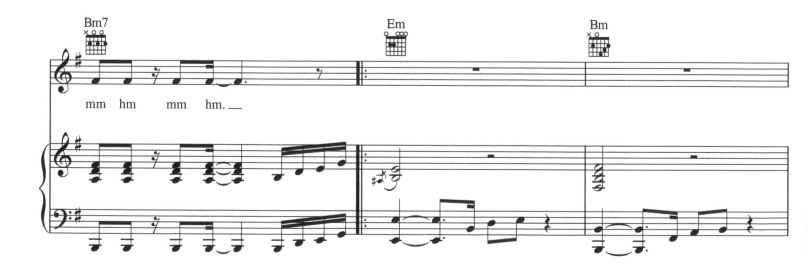

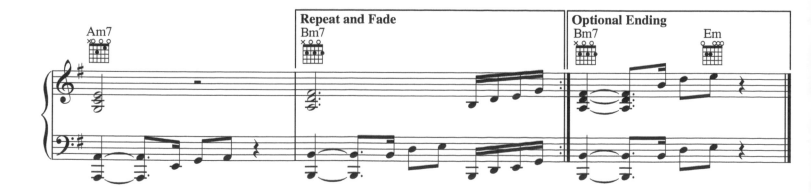

YOU DON'T KNOW MY NAME

Words and Music by ALICIA KEYS,
KANYE OMARI WEST, HAROLD SPENCER LILLY,
J.R. BAILEY, MEL KENT and KEN WILLIAMS

'cause not a lot of guys are worth__ my time,_____ oh._____
And ooh,__ it set__ my soul__ on fire._____

Ooh,__ ba-by, ba-by, ba - by,__ it's get-tin' kind-a cra - zy_____
Ooh,__ ba-by, ba-by, ba - by,__ I can't wait__ for the first time._____

'cause you are tak - in' o - ver my mind._____ And it feels__ like
My i-mag-i-na-tion's run - nin'__ wild._____ It feels__ like

ooh, _____ you don't know my ___

___ name. I swear _____ it feels ___ like

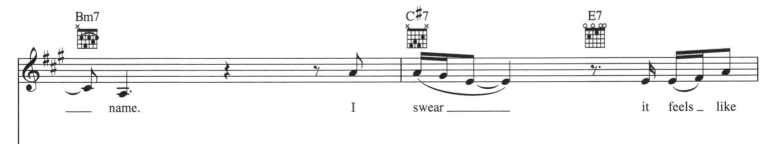

ooh, _____ you don't know my ___

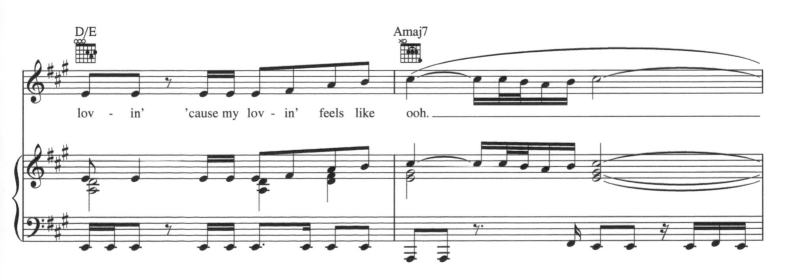

Spoken Lyrics

I might have to just go ahead and call this boy.
Hello, can I speak to, to, Michael? Oh, hey, how you doin'?
Uh, I feel kinda silly doin' this but um, this is the waitress from the coffee house on 39th and Lenox.
You know, the one with the braids. Yeah, well I see you on Wednesdays all the time.
You come in every Wednesday on your lunch break, I think, and you always order the special with the hot chocolate.
My manager be trippin' and stuff talkin' 'bout we gotta use water but I always use some milk and cream for you 'cause,
I think you're kinda sweet.
Anyway, you always got on some fly, blue suit, mmm.
Your cuff links are shinin' all bright. So what you do?
Oh, word. Yeah that's interesting.
Look man, I mean I don't wanna waste your time but I know girls don't usually do this.
But I was wonderin' if maybe we could get together outside the restaurant one day?
You know, 'cause I do look a lot different outside my work clothes.
I mean, we could just go across the street to the park right here.
Wait, hold up, my - my cell phone breakin' up.
Can you hear me now? Yeah, so what day did you say?
Oh, Thursday's perfect.

THE ULTIMATE SONGBOOKS

HAL•LEONARD®
PIANO PLAY-ALONG

AUDIO ACCESS INCLUDED

These great songbooks come with our standard arrangements for piano and voice with guitar chord frames plus audio.

Each book includes either a CD or access to online recordings of full performance of each song, as well as a second track without the piano part so you can play "lead" with the band!

HAL•LEONARD®

Visit Hal Leonard Online at
www.halleonard.com

Prices, contents and availability
subject to change without notice.

PEANUTS © United Feature Syndicate, Inc.
Disney Characters and Artwork ™ © 2019 Disney

* Audio contains backing tracks only.

PLAY PIANO LIKE A PRO!

AMAZING PHRASING – KEYBOARD
50 Ways to Improve Your Improvisational Skills
by Debbie Denke

Amazing Phrasing is for any keyboard player interested in learning how to improvise and how to improve their creative phrasing. This method is divided into three parts: melody, harmony, and rhythm & style. The online audio contains 44 full-band demos for listening, as well as many play-along examples so you can practice improvising over various musical styles and progressions.
00842030 Book/Online Audio... $16.99

BEBOP LICKS FOR PIANO
A Dictionary of Melodic Ideas for Improvisation
by Les Wise

Written for the musician who is interested in acquiring a firm foundation for playing jazz, this unique book/audio pack presents over 800 licks. By building up a vocabulary of these licks, players can connect them together in endless possibilities to form larger phrases and complete solos. The book includes piano notation, and the online audio contains helpful note-for-note demos of every lick.
00311854 Book/Online Audio... $17.99

BOOGIE WOOGIE FOR BEGINNERS
by Frank Paparelli

A short easy method for learning to play boogie woogie, designed for the beginner and average pianist. Includes: exercises for developing left-hand bass • 25 popular boogie woogie bass patterns • arrangements of "Down the Road a Piece" and "Answer to the Prayer" by well-known pianists • a glossary of musical terms for dynamics, tempo and style.
00120517 .... $10.99

HAL LEONARD JAZZ PIANO METHOD
by Mark Davis

This is a comprehensive and easy-to-use guide designed for anyone interested in playing jazz piano – from the complete novice just learning the basics to the more advanced player who wishes to enhance their keyboard vocabulary. The accompanying audio includes demonstrations of all the examples in the book! Topics include essential theory, chords and voicings, improvisation ideas, structure and forms, scales and modes, rhythm basics, interpreting a lead sheet, playing solos, and much more!
00131102 Book/Online Audio... $19.99

INTROS, ENDINGS & TURNAROUNDS FOR KEYBOARD
Essential Phrases for Swing, Latin, Jazz Waltz, and Blues Styles
by John Valerio

Learn the intros, endings and turnarounds that all of the pros know and use! This new keyboard instruction book by John Valerio covers swing styles, ballads, Latin tunes, jazz waltzes, blues, major and minor keys, vamps and pedal tones, and more.
00290525 .... $12.99

JAZZ PIANO TECHNIQUE
Exercises, Etudes & Ideas for Building Chops
by John Valerio

This one-of-a-kind book applies traditional technique exercises to specific jazz piano needs. Topics include: scales (major, minor, chromatic, pentatonic, etc.), arpeggios (triads, seventh chords, upper structures), finger independence exercises (static position, held notes, Hanon exercises), parallel interval scales and exercises (thirds, fourths, tritones, fifths, sixths, octaves), and more! The online audio includes 45 recorded examples.
00312059 Book/Online Audio... $19.99

JAZZ PIANO VOICINGS
An Essential Resource for Aspiring Jazz Musicians
by Rob Mullins

The jazz idiom can often appear mysterious and difficult for musicians who were trained to play other types of music. Long-time performer and educator Rob Mullins helps players enter the jazz world by providing voicings that will help the player develop skills in the jazz genre and start sounding professional right away – without years of study! Includes a "Numeric Voicing Chart," chord indexes in all 12 keys, info about what range of the instrument you can play chords in, and a beginning approach to bass lines.
00310914 .... $19.99

OSCAR PETERSON – JAZZ EXERCISES, MINUETS, ETUDES & PIECES FOR PIANO
Legendary jazz pianist Oscar Peterson has long been devoted to the education of piano students. In this book he offers dozens of pieces designed to empower the student, whether novice or classically trained, with the technique needed to become an accomplished jazz pianist.
00311225 .... $14.99

PIANO AEROBICS
by Wayne Hawkins

Piano Aerobics is a set of exercises that introduces students to many popular styles of music, including jazz, salsa, swing, rock, blues, new age, gospel, stride, and bossa nova. In addition, there is a online audio with accompaniment tracks featuring professional musicians playing in those styles.
00311863 Book/Online Audio $19.99

PIANO FITNESS
A Complete Workout
by Mark Harrison

This book will give you a thorough technical workout, while having fun at the same time! The accompanying online audio allows you to play along with a rhythm section as you practice your scales, arpeggios, and chords in all keys. Instead of avoiding technique exercises because they seem too tedious or difficult, you'll look forward to playing them. Various voicings and rhythmic settings, which are extremely useful in a variety of pop and jazz styles, are also introduced.
00311995 Book/Online Audio... $19.99

HAL•LEONARD®
7777 W. BLUEMOUND RD. P.O. BOX 13819
MILWAUKEE, WISCONSIN 53213
www.halleonard.com

Prices, contents, and availability subject to change without notice.